GW00362837

PORT OF PLYMOUTH
S E R I E S

Merchant Shipping

PORT OF PLYMOUTH
S E R I E S
Merchant Shipping

Martin Langley and Edwina Small

DEVON BOOKS

This book is part of a series which together form a history of the Port of Plymouth. Subject to demand it is hoped to publish, not necessarily in numerical order, the complete set of books comprising this project.

First published in Great Britain in 1988 by Devon Books

Copyright © Martin Langley & Edwina Small, 1988

ISBN: 0 86114-805-3

British Library Cataloguing-in-Publication Data
Langley, Martin
  Merchant shipping at Plymouth.—(Port of Plymouth series).
  1. Shipping—England—Plymouth(Devon)— History—19th Century
  2. Shipping—England—Plymouth(Devon)—History—20th Century
  I. Title   II. Small, Edwina   III. Series
  387.5' 09423' 58   HE825

Printed and bound in Great Britain by A. Wheaton & Co. Ltd.

DEVON BOOKS

Official Publisher to Devon County Council
An imprint of Wheaton Publishers Ltd, a member of Maxwell Pergamon Publishing Corporation plc

Wheaton Publishers Ltd
Hennock Road, Marsh Barton, Exeter, Devon EX2 8RP
Tel: 0392 74121; Telex 42749 (WHEATN G)

SALES

Direct sales enquiries to Devon Books at the address above.
Trade sales to: Town & Country Books, P.O. Box 31, Newton Abbot, Devon TQ12 5AQ. Tel: 08047 2690

To
Captain Stan Daymond
former master of the tug *Boarhound*

Acknowledgements

J.F.O. Browning of West Hoe
Stan Daymond of Mutley
W.R. Eddison of Plymstock
Rufus Endle of Plymstock
Bill Jackson of Peverell
C.J. Low, M.B.E. of Ford Park
Ernest Rogers of Greenbank
Tom Stroud of Higher Compton
Alfred Tope of Prince Rock
Ronald Vosper of Crownhill

Also, from farther afield:
W.M. Benn of Exmouth
Capt. J.A. Simpson of Largs
R.C. Trace of Newport

Bristol Central Library
Cornish Shipping Co. Ltd
National Maritime Museum
Plymouth Shipping Co. (G.E. Monsen)
Plymouth Central Library
Southampton Central Library

Illustrations are reproduced by permission of the following:

Terry W. Belt: p. 8;
Jim Broad: p. 9;
Dermot Fitzgerald: p. 25;
S.V. Goodman: pp. 13,22,23;
Bill Jackson: p. 4;
Martin Langley: p.26;
Graham Langmuir: p. 16;
National Maritime Museum: p. 2;
Michael Parsons: p. 27;
Edwina Small: p. 5;
Sutton Harbour Company: p. 18;
Western Morning News: pp. 19,20,31,33.

Merchant Shipping

SHIPS FROM NEAR AND FAR

A photograph in the possession of the National Maritime Museum, taken in 1850, shows part of a great assemblage of 300 merchant sailing ships sheltering, windbound, in Plymouth Sound. Although less than 140 years ago, and not such an unusual scene at the time, today it seems well-nigh unbelievable. Most of the vessels shown are of humble size, employed in the home and continental trade. Brigs, brigantines, sloops and small barques had long been the traditional coasters, but were already giving place to schooners, and by the 1870s, to ketches. Throughout the nineteenth century and indeed until the Second World War there was a strong and vigorous coastal trade: and the schooners and ketches which maintained it until steam took over far outnumbered the great foreign-going barques and full-rigged ships. So also it was the merchant schooners and their humbler sisters the barges of the Tamar which in their day dominated Plymouth's seaborne commerce.

DEEP-SEA TRAFFIC

However, in those days when sail reigned supreme, there were also constant arrivals of deep-sea ships at Plymouth from every part of the world. Foreshadowing the ocean liners of the heyday of steam were the American sailing packets running between Plymouth and New York in the 1820s and 1830s. Among these were the *Westminster* and *St Leonard* which provided the fastest passages then obtainable.

But the deep-sea traffic was not only transatlantic. The port registers often betray how far Plymouth's own ships worked from home when deregistration is recorded as due to wreck. There was the brigantine *Speculation*. Formerly a French warship, taken as prize by H.M.S. *Bittern*, she was acquired by Thomas Billing of Devonport and registered at Plymouth in 1826. Her end came in 1829 when she was destroyed by fire on the Newfoundland coast, the register stating: 'No account of the master and

Some of 300 merchant sailing ships, sheltering windbound in Plymouth Sound, 1850 – not an unusual sight at the time.

crew has been received, and the register was lost with the ship.' There was the 441 ton barque *Carshalton Park*. Built at Southampton in 1811, she was bought from London owners by three Plymouth partners in 1850, Captain W.S. Blair being appointed master. She was wrecked off the distant shores of Sierra Leone in 1853. The full-rigged ship *Siam* (721 tons, 151 ft overall), built in 1852 in Nova Scotia, was bought by Plymouth merchants two years later. Her Plymouth registration was cancelled in 1856 when she ran ashore at St Catherine's Island, Savannah, and became a total loss. The 162 ft barque *Jessie Boyle* was acquired by five Plymouth merchants in 1869. Built at St John's, New Brunswick in 1854, the *Jessie Boyle* was wrecked off Cape Holandes, on the south coast of Cuba. With Australia, too, Plymouth was in regular communication by sea. Joseph Conrad (1857 – 1924) who later gained fame as a maritime novelist, served as mate in the clipper *Torrens* when she made a passage from Plymouth to Adelaide in ninety-five days in 1891. The 221 ft *Torrens*, of 1875, was on the Australia run for twenty-eight years.

PLYMOUTH FLEETS

Most of Plymouth's sail freighters were singly operated, often part-owned by their skippers; but in the latter half of the nineteenth century there were several Plymouth fleets in being. William Pinkham & Co. (1860s – 80s) owned a number of large deep-sea vessels, including the tops'l schooner *Polly Pinkham* (1867), *Kitty Pinkham*, *Eschol* (1870), and the brigantine *Amy*, all built by Mansfield's of Teignmouth and engaged in ocean trade to South America. From the 1870s well into the present century W.H. Shilston & Co. had a fleet in general deep-sea trades and later also fetched Newfoundland salted cod for European ports. Their vessels varied from barques and barquentines to small schooners and were mostly built on their own slips. Two were lost at sea: the schooner *Girl of Devon* (131 tons) disappeared without trace in 1905, and the barquentine *Countess of Devon* (213 tons) sank in a storm in Liverpool Bay two years later.

From the 1880s till the 1930s the Westcotts of Sutton Pool had a fleet of well-maintained schooners and ketches engaged in both overseas and home trade. The story of this fleet is told in detail by Ian D. Merry in *The Westcotts and Their Times*, a National Maritime Museum monograph of 1977. The schooner *Western Lass* sailed originally under Shilston's flag and later for Westcott's. In November 1916 she stranded near Start Point and the Salcombe lifeboat was called out. The boat arrived to find that the schooner's crew had been rescued by Prawle Rocket Brigade and on return from her fruitless journey she was capsized on the harbour bar, all but two of the lifeboatmen losing their lives. The *Western Lass* survived this catastrophe,

The Plymouth owned three-masted tops'l schooner Carmenta *(144 tons) in 1921. She was wrecked three years later.*

being refloated and towed to Plymouth. Sold to Westcott's the following year she continued trading till July 1927, when, bound for Glasgow with china clay, she was becalmed in dense fog off Cape Cornwall, drifted on to the Brisons, and was wrecked.

At the turn of the century the Plymouth Mercantile Shipping Co. operated a brigantine, two schooners, two ketches and two smacks. Their largest vessel was the 125 ton brigantine *Snowdrop*, built in 1873 in the Channel Islands. Their smack *JNR*, Kingsbridge-built in 1893 is still afloat, restored, privately owned, and kept on the Tamar at Weir Quay. Her name derives from the initials of her first owner, James Nicholson Roose. Her last commercial service was salvaging gear from the wreck of H.M.S. *Warspite* in 1947.

In the early years of this century Davis & Stephens owned a small fleet of ketches which included the still-remembered *Alfred Rooker* (1876). She came to the fleet with an already established reputation as the fastest boat on the Corunna cattle run. After some years in the Newfoundland cod trade, she survived a stranding at Cherbourg and completed fifty-eight years of service before being abandoned in Hooelake, where her remains lie today. Her name was that of the Mayor of Plymouth in the year of her launch. For some years she was skippered by Ernest Tope who had formerly commanded the *Amethyst* in the same fleet. His elder brother, Alfred Tope, was skipper of Davis & Stephens' 39 ton ketch *Britannia*, sunk by U-boat in 1916 north of Alderney, and his cousin Albert was captain of *Regina*, another Davis & Stephens' vessel.

The Topes were a Plymouth seafaring family of whom three became shipowners – Alfred and his cousins, the brothers William and Jack. The Tope family ships did not operate as a fleet but were independently owned and run. Alfred Tope, after serving his time with Davis and Stephens, became owner/skipper of the 120 ton tops'l schooner *Dolphin* in 1916, with his nephew Bill Jackson as mate. The *Dolphin* traded principally up and down the west coast, with clay outward, coal returning. She came unscathed through the Great War, despite numerous crossings of the Channel unescorted. Today her remains, with the large sternpost still standing, lie on the north shore of Hooelake. In 1921 Alfred Tope bought the three-masted schooner *Carmenta*, but three years later she was wrecked on Liverpool bar, fortunately without loss of life.

From 1904 – 15 Alfred's cousin William Tope was owner/skipper of the *Twilight*, a large Hull deep-sea trawler converted at Plymouth for coastal trading. In 1915 he took over the Guernsey ketch *Louise Ernest*, only to lose her in unusual circumstances three years later. Entering Dover harbour in a

Tops'l schooner Dolphin, *120 tons, c.1923. From a painting in the possession of her former mate. One of the Tope family ships, her remains are now buried at Hooelake.*

gale in late 1918, she struck the wreck of H.M.S. *Glatton,* a coast defence monitor which had blown up on 16 September that year. Leaking badly, the *Louise Ernest* was towed by the tug *Lady Brassey* into Dover inner harbour, and run ashore on impetus. Her bow struck the wall heavily and the additional damage put her beyond economic repair. She was uninsured and though salvage craft soon lifted the wreck, she had to be sold for scrap. William's brother, Jack Tope, was owner/skipper of the ketch *Cicilia* from 1917 to about 1923 and employed his second cousin Bill Tope as mate. *Cicilia* mounted a gun on her foredeck during the Great War.

The Roose family owned the last Plymouth sail fleet, but with the exception of their 'flagship', the 87 ton schooner *Hector Candy* (ex Cecil Brindley), their six vessels were small and confined to coastal and inshore work.

PLYMOUTH SAIL FREIGHTERS

A vast number of merchant sailing ships were built, registered or owned in Plymouth during the last century, while many more were associated with the port in their regular trade. Only a few can be mentioned here.

The ketch *Charlotte* was built at Plymouth in 1840, and worked from the port until sold to the Harris fleet at Appledore in 1900. Her deadweight capacity was 80 tons.

The barque *Serena,* 472 tons, was launched at Birkenhead in 1864, as the *Eivir.* Owned by Plymouth merchant Thomas Symons, she survived till about 1905 and was probably the last barque to be Plymouth owned and registered.

The brigantine *Ariel* (1864, 132 tons) built, registered and owned at Plymouth had a life of over forty years, but finished her days working out of Padstow.

The three-masted schooner *Ann Wheaton* (228 tons) built in 1865 by Elias Cox of Bridport was Plymouth registered and Plymouth owned. She was of partly composite construction, and built for the deep-water trade.

The brigantine *Margaret Sutton,* 171 tons, traded under the flag of Thomas Steer, Plymouth, until at least 1903, but had been Irish built in 1866.

The topsail schooner *Elizabeth Drew* (built Padstow 1871) was Plymouth registered and Plymouth based, and employed in the Newfoundland salted-codfish trade for about seventeen years. After a spell in Cornish hands she returned to Plymouth ownership in 1909. Her end came in July 1933, long after she had left the port, when lying windbound in the Downs, she was run down and cut in two by a German motor freighter.

The ketch *Winifred* (38 tons) of 1874 was generally typical of small West Country ketches, but had a running bowsprit and was fitted with a special windlass. Her remains, damaged by fire, can be seen in Old Mill Creek on the Dart.

The barquentine *Frances & Jane*, 212 tons, had been built at Harwich in 1878. Registered and owned in Plymouth, she was trading deep-sea for many years including a spell in the Newfoundland codfish trade. She ended her days in Itchenor Creek as a houseboat.

The schooner *Carrie Harvey* (1881) built and registered at Plymouth, was owned by a Mr Trevaskis. Her gross tonnage was 111. Before the First World War she was skippered by C. Carrieslake.

The ketch *Clara May* (150 tons deadweight) was launched in Millbay Docks in 1891. She was registered at Plymouth throughout her career, though owned successively in Somerset, Suffolk, Cornwall and Devon. After sixty-two years' service, she was laid up in Braunton Pill in 1953, succumbing to a fire a year or so later.

FREQUENT CALLERS

Among merchant sailing vessels which called fairly frequently at Plymouth, the following were perhaps the best known.

The schooner *Rhoda Mary* (1868, 130 tons) was renowned for her fast passages. In the 1870s when bringing coal from South Shields to Plymouth in company with other schooners she had berthed and discharged her cargo before the others arrived. Many who knew her well were sure that she was the fastest trading schooner ever built in Britain. She lasted in hulk form until the Second World War when she was abandoned in the Medway and left to rot.

The tops'l schooner *Millom Castle* (1870, 93 tons) was a good sea boat and very handy to sail either laden or in ballast. After forty-two years' service for the Postlethwaite fleet in Cumberland she was sold to Slade's of Appledore and later cut down to ketch rig and given an auxiliary motor. When bringing coal to Devonport Dockyard in October 1932 she suffered severe storm damage, was brought in by the lifeboat, and did not go to sea again. Her dismasted hull can be seen at Poldrissick, on the River Lynher.

The small ketch *Rob Roy* (1882, 23 tons) brought mature oysters from Helford River for Plymouth market. In 1905 she was sold, renamed *Ailsie* and later motorized. In 1925 she was lost at sea: there were no survivors.

The three-masted tops'l schooner *Alert* (1885, 133 tons) registered at Falmouth, began life as a Newfoundland trader, and later carried granite from Cornwall for the construction of the mole at Gibraltar. After the First World War she used to bring coal for the Devonport Gas Co., berthing at Pottery Quay in the Hamoaze. She was not withdrawn until 1938.

The steel tops'l schooner *Result* (1893, 122 tons) distinguished herself in the

The three-masted schooner *Natal* from Port Natal, for London, put into Plymouth. She brings 18 passengers and a full cargo of wood, ivory, and other Colonial products, and has been 77 days on her passage.
WESTERN MORNING NEWS,
26 September 1865

Tops'l schooner Volant *of Kirkwall (113 tons, 1875) at anchor off the Cattewater on 4 August 1933. She had a 21 h.p. auxiliary engine.*

Ketch Amazon *of Barnstaple (49 tons) at Plymouth on 15 November 1934. Two years later she stranded off Picklecombe Fort, but was towed off. Her bones lie today in Hooelake.*

Great War when, having been commandeered by the Navy, she was used as a Q-ship and was twice in action with German U-boats. She became a regular visitor to Plymouth, bringing coal to Torpoint for Reynolds' tugs, and general cargoes to Sutton Harbour. She remained in trade till 1967, was then restored to original condition by Harland & Wolf, Belfast, and is now on display at the Ulster Folk & Transport Museum, Cultra, Co. Down.

The tops'l schooner *Kathleen & May* (1900, 147 tons) was a regular caller at Plymouth in the eight years after her launch under her original name of *Lizzie May*. She survived at least four collisions to become one of the last four coastal schooners under the Red Ensign. Withdrawn in 1960, she was acquired and restored by the Maritime Trust, and opened to the public in Sutton Harbour, Plymouth in 1972. Insufficient patronage occasioned her removal in 1979 to her present resting-place in St Katherine's Dock, London.

The barquentine *Rigdin* (1907, 311 tons) was built in Finland as a topsail schooner named *Ingrid*, of which *Rigdin* was an anagram bestowed under British ownership. When she became uneconomic for deep-sea work, she was put into the home trade, but her deep draught and length of over 140 feet were against her. It was in those days that she was quite frequently in Plymouth and it was to Plymouth that she came at last to die. Towed from Fowey, where she had lain derelict, she was anchored in the Cattewater to await the breakers and sank at her moorings.

THE TAMAR BARGES

No record of the merchant sail era at Plymouth would be complete without reference to the smacks and Tamar barges. These were the maids-of-all work of the estuary waters. They had developed from the primitive market boats of the eighteenth century into well-designed and very stoutly built craft loading, according to their size, from 40 to 70 tons of cargo and giving usually over forty years of arduous service to their owners.

The smaller craft, of 20 to 30 tons gross, were often referred to as 'inside' barges and worked within harbour limits, rarely going outside the Breakwater except perhaps to Cawsand. The larger barges, often ketch-rigged and varying from 30 to 50 tons gross, regularly worked down the coast to Fowey, the Fal and beyond, and occasionally up-Channel as far as Dartmouth.

Their hulls were mostly built of English oak on elm keels, with pitchpine decks. They were crewed by just two men – master and mate, the master expecting to be known as 'Captain'. In spite of some of the filthy cargoes they were required to carry – gravel, ores, manure – it was their pride to keep the aft cabin highly varnished, and spotlessly clean; indeed a typical barge cabin could vie with any Romany caravan.

Well-known among the 'outside' or seagoing barges were the following:

Mayblossom (1889, 34 tons). In her early days voyaged as far afield as Southampton and Guernsey. Working till 1950, when laid up in Turnpike Creek, Falmouth, where her remains were buried under rubble when road developments were carried out in 1981.

The Sirdar (1899, 40 tons). Named after Kitchener, victor of Omdurman that year. 70 tons capacity. Served as a balloon-barrage vessel in the Second World War. Sold to Lisbon 1947; believed sunk soon after.

Shortest Day (1870, 40 tons). Ketch-rigged. Believed to be the barge depicted rounding the Impham Turn in a local postcard of Morwell Rocks. Her last voyage was to Dittisham Creek where she was broken up. Her rudder can still be seen there.

Well-known among the 'inside' barges were:

Emm (1883, 22½ tons). Variously employed over the years; carrying stone to Torpoint, sand-dredging up the Plym, and ferrying cement and infill to the Breakwater. Scrapped *c.* 1950.

Flora May (1897, 22 tons). Owned until 1918 by Captain C.A. Daymond; taken over by the Navy that year. Subsequent fate unknown.

By the 1920s the barges were fighting for survival, and most sacrificed cabin and hold space to instal an engine and become more competitive: but rail and road transport steadily took away their cargoes, and by the Second World War commercial sailing craft on Plymouth rivers were only a memory. Two Tamar barges are preserved and afloat today. The JNR (1893, 41 tons) has been maintained in good order privately, and her owner lives aboard her at Weir Quay. The *Shamrock* (1899, 32 tons) has been restored by the National Trust and National Maritime Museum, after being towed in a derelict state from Hooelake to Cotehele Quay, where she is now on view to the public. The recognizable remains of two other barges lie in the River Lynher. The complete hull, dismasted, of the *Lynher* (1896, 29 tons) lies at Poldrissick Quarry quay, alongside the old schooner *Millom Castle*, while the hulk of a barge at Forder Creek has been variously identified as *Lord Roberts*, *Saltash*, or *Village Belle*. A praiseworthy venture for any enthusiast to whom money is a secondary consideration would be the salvaging and restoration of the *Lynher* – a more typical Tamar barge than the *Shamrock* – and her display in the setting of the ore quays at Morwellham. A comprehensive study and list of Plymouth barges is published by the National Maritime Museum, entitled *The Shipping and Trade of the River Tamar* (Parts 1 and 2) by Ian D. Merry (Monograph no. 46).

It is a little-known fact that the steam whistles or sirens of steamships were a Plymouth invention. In 1826 inventor Adrian Stephens connected a device to a steam boiler to tell him audibly when steam was escaping.

FROM SAIL TO STEAM

Deep-sea sailing ships were trading in and out of Plymouth until the late 1930s, mostly foreign owned, such as the Latvian timber ships which came to Sutton Pool, and occasionally the Finnish barques and full-rigged ships under Eriksson's flag. A few came to grief: a barque whose name is unrecorded was towed off the Breakwater about 1908 by the tug *Triumph*, and the French barquentine *Yvonne* became a wreck there in 1920. But the expansion of trade and travel brought about by the Industrial Revolution demanded not only the reliability of engine power at sea, but an increase in the size and capacity of ships, and this factor more than any other hastened the end of the sailing ship. Increased size meant more sail area, involving yards and spars too unwieldy to be smartly handled. It also required iron hulls for commensurate strength: the proportion of iron ships to wooden ones built in Britain increased from one-third in 1860 to five-sixths in 1870. By 1865 British yards were building more steamships than sailing vessels. The first steamships seen at Plymouth came in 1815, the year of Waterloo. In June that year the paddler *Thomas* called, on the first open-sea voyage of any British steamer, and later the paddler *Duke of Argyle*, on passage from the Clyde to London.

STEAM COASTERS

The home trade steam coaster soon began to make inroads into the coal, ore, and cattle-carrying trades of the merchant schooners. By 1826 there were wooden paddle freighters working between Britain and Portugal, and where short-distance voyages made frequent coaling possible, steam coasters could pay their way. However it was not until the paddle had given place to the screw, and the simple engine had been superseded by the compound and the triple-expansion, that they developed rapidly – though for some years still rigged with fore-and-aft sails – until three principal types of steam coaster emerged by about 1880: (a) engines amidships, holds fore and aft, about 230 ft length o.a.; (b) engines aft, bridge amidships between holds, about 140 ft – 160 ft length o.a.; (c) engines and bridge aft, hold/holds for'ard, about 90 ft – 140 ft length o.a. Engines-amidships vessels were much less numerous than the engines-aft types in coastal trading, where loading and discharging were frequent. Fore-and-aft trim was always a problem when loading, and the shaft-tunnel in the after hold restricted the use of crane grabs when discharging.

Although steam coasters could have afforded better living conditions for their crews than merchant schooners, such was scarcely the case. Seamen (to starb'd) and firemen (to port) lived either side of a fore-and-aft partition in the fo'c'sle, which often also accommodated a lamp room, paint locker and crew's toilet. Coal-fired bogey stoves provided the only heating. Captain and mates had cabins under the bridge, and the engineers above the engine-room, but while the officers fared better for privacy, their cabins had no refinements. The bridge was usually an open affair with only a canvas dodger to afford shelter against the weather. All steam coasters had reciprocating engines, and by 1890 could manage about 8½ – 9 knots on a fuel consumption of ½ oz of coal per ton per mile steamed. They also had a steam steering engine, linked to the rudder quadrant by rod and chain, with relieving tackle to absorb excessive kicking by the rudder in rough seas. The hatches of the ship's cargo holds were covered by stout tarpaulins stretched over wooden beams and secured by hatch-bars and wedges. Mast derricks and steam-driven cargo winches enabled coasters to handle their own cargoes where quayside cranes were lacking. Almost until the Second World War most steam coasters had no radio, so did not receive weather reports. Life-saving equipment usually comprised two oar-and-lugs'l lifeboats in radial davits, two bridge lifebuoys with acetylene flares, enough kapok lifejackets for the ship's company, and a small supply of distress rockets.

M.V. Hibernian Coast, *ex* Aberdeen Coast *(1258 tons, 1946) arriving at Plymouth on 27 June 1958. She was a regular caller until sold in 1968.*

FROM STEAM TO DIESEL

Merchant schooner building virtually ceased in 1910 and until the Second World War the steam coaster reigned supreme in coastwise trade. Decline began in the 1930s, when reliable diesels became available for this class of vessel. The Dutch, who favoured the oil engine for its savings on manning,

fuel and engine weight, began to offer very strong competition. After the war, when many steam coasters fell victim to mines, the decline continued, and today the only British steam coaster surviving in home waters is the *Robin* (1890, 400 tons), preserved at St Katherine's Dock, London by the Maritime Trust. The subject of British steam coasters has been comprehensively reviewed in *Steam Coasters and Short Sea Traders* by C.V. Waine (1979) and *Old Time Steam Coasting* by Spargo and Thomason (1982), both published by Waine Research Publications. The first merchant motor vessel registered in Plymouth was in 1905.

FREQUENT CALLERS

A number of steam coasters which were frequent callers at Plymouth will be referred to elsewhere in this series in the books on the various harbours. Some worth mentioning here include the *Daisy* (1898, 555 tons) and other steamers of the 'Flower line' (Richard Hughes of Liverpool) bringing coal and taking away stone or china clay; the small tramps of F.T. Everard & Sons, with general cargoes; the *Carrowdale* and other coasters of A. Guinness, Son & Co., who brought Guinness in casks to Plymouth from Dublin every Monday, while carrying a part-cargo for London; and the S.S. *Flathouse* (1931, 1546 tons) of the Powell-Duffryn fleet, bringing gas coal to Plymouth gasworks. There were the ships of Bain, Sons & Co. of Portreath, seen often at Plymouth between 1890 and 1925, especially the S.S. *Test* (1890, 466 tons) which discharged cement at Plymouth every Thursday – Friday, sailing Friday night to Guernsey where she loaded coal for London, and leaving the Thames with cement for Plymouth again on the Monday.

Some of the best-remembered coasters were the *Force* ships of the West Coast Shipping Co. (W.S. Kennaugh & Co.). The Kennaughs took a pride in keeping their vessels clean and in first-class condition. They had a colour scheme of grey hull with a white line separating the red boot-topping, and a buff funnel. Whenever Kennaugh ships returned to their home port, Liverpool, their crews saw to it that paintwork and varnish were beyond reproach. Of the twenty-one steamers owned by the company over the years, three, strangely, were lost when making for Plymouth. On 12 July 1929 the *Aira Force* (1891, 349 tons) which by then had been sold to Alfred J. Smith Ltd, was sunk in collision in the Bristol Channel whilst on a voyage from Cardiff to Plymouth with a cargo of flour. On 8 April 1940 the *Holme Force* (1930, 1216 tons) was torpedoed and sunk by E boat off Newhaven while on passage from Tynemouth to Plymouth with coal for Pottery Quay; ten crew were saved. On 21 November 1948 the *Colwith Force* (1918, 805 tons) stranded and capsized in the River Ouse whilst on passage from Goole to Plymouth with coal.

COAST LINES LIMITED
WEEKLY CARGO SERVICE BETWEEN
LIVERPOOL, LONDON, DUBLIN, BELFAST AND PLYMOUTH

STEVEDORING - WAREHOUSING
STOCK-KEEPING - ROAD DELIVERY

Berths available for vessels up to 20 feet in draught, always afloat.

Rail connected quays.   Cranage facilities.

Extensive warehouse accommodation.

VICTORIA WHARVES
PLYMOUTH PHONE: 63175

Coastal liners Western Coast *(left) and* Southern Coast *side by side at Victoria Wharves in the 1930s. Carrying general cargo and some passengers they were on a round-the-British-Isles timetable service, one eastbound, the other westbound.*

There were also the smaller vessels of Coast Lines Ltd which did not run timetable services but carried out coastwise tramping. These were *Devon Coast* (1909, 782 tons), *Dorset Coast* (1924, 483 tons) and *Kentish Coast* (1908, 758 tons). The wreck of the last-named in Plymouth Sound will be recorded in a subsequent book on Plymouth Towage.

PLYMOUTH COMPANIES

With the introduction of powered ships, Plymouth ceased, with two exceptions, to be a base port for coasters. The exceptions were the Plym Shipping Co. Ltd (A.E. Monson), which was trading with steam coasters from the mid-forties till 1958, and the Cornish Shipping Co. Ltd (Sanders Stevens & Co.), which is still operating six motor coasters. The Plym Shipping Co. were trading chiefly to Continental ports between the Elbe and Brest, with occasional voyages into the Baltic for timber. Some ships ran on charter for a number of years between London and Paris, and between Weymouth and the Channel Islands for British Rail. The steamers, which had a black funnel with white band, ceased trading because British regulations required manning levels which inhibited competition with

Dutch, Danish and German ships of similar size. The Cornish Shipping Co., which owns four motor coasters and manages two others, handles general cargoes to and from North European ports between the Bay of Biscay and the Baltic, especially clay, fertilizers, and steel. Funnel and flag colours are blue with a white logo. Their M.V. *Roy Clemo* made news in 1980 when she rescued the crew of a sinking Weymouth fishing boat.

STEAM ON THE HIGH SEAS

The deep-sea steamer could not at first compete successfully with the sailing vessel. It consumed prodigious quantities of fuel, and bunker-space reduced cargo capacity. Only the granting of mail contracts by the government made it possible for the deep-sea steamers to pay their way. 'The steam packet ... paved the way for the steamship.' This situation was changed, initially by the advent of the compound engine in 1864, and supremely by triple-expansion in 1880. The successful voyage of the triple-expansion S.S. *Aberdeen* from Plymouth to Australia on 7 April 1881 sounded the death-knell of the big sailing ships.

CARGO LINERS

From the mid nineteenth century to the mid twentieth century deep-sea merchant steamers were of three principal classes: cargo liners, tramps and passenger liners. British cargo liners which carried at least twelve passengers, became ubiquitous: they served the indiscriminate import and export trade not only of Great Britain, but of the world. Plymouth, however, saw little of them. They were often vessels of 8000 tons or more gross and 450 ft in length, requiring deep-water berths, while many were purpose-built for one kind of cargo and their owners preferred quays with sophisticated loading and discharging plant. However, the Strick Line (1923) Ltd of London regularly brought barley to Plymouth from Bhandur Shapoor in the Persian Gulf in the cargo liners *Tabaristan* (1914, 6251 tons), *Floristan* (1928, 5378 tons) and Nigaristan (1912, 5993 tons), the last named calling about every six weeks. The company traded between Britain, the Mediterranean, the Red Sea, North Africa and U.S. ports. The largest merchant vessels ever registered in Plymouth were in fact cargo and intermediate liners – the Maori-named ships of the New Zealand Shipping Co. Ltd, which ran from London and/or Southampton to New Zealand via the Panama Canal. Latterly they called at Plymouth only on outward voyages, picking up the last mail and sometimes signing a crew replacement brought off in a launch by the shipping agents. The company had a long association with Plymouth, and all their liners were Plymouth-registered, even those based in New Zealand. This was no doubt in tribute to the original colonization of New Zealand by

On board the steamship *Norham Castle*, Captain A. Winchester, which arrived in Plymouth last night, a fatal accident occurred two days after the ship left the Cape. An able seaman, named Smith, was assisting in stowing the foresail. He was kneeling on the yard when he lost his balance and pitched on his head on the forecastle.
WESTERN MORNING NEWS,
23 September 1885

S.S. Hastings *(Capt. G.N. Natson) berthed in Sutton Harbour. Believed to be a 1904 picture of the ship when she called for provisioning and coaling en route for Rangoon, where she spent her working life.*

The cargo liner American Merchant **anchored in the Sound, January 1933. On her crossing of the Atlantic she had gone to the assistance of the sinking** Exeter City.

ships from Plymouth in 1839 and 1840. The American Merchant Line were once-a-year callers until 1936 sending a cargo liner to pick up Channel Island cattle for America, the Channel Island cattlemen accompanying them. The trans-shipment was done in Plymouth Sound, from freighters direct from Guernsey. From 150 to 200 cattle would be loaded by slings, cows sometimes calving as a result!

DEEP-SEA TRAMPS

Deep-sea tramps far outnumbered the cargo liners before the Great War. The tramp ship was pre-eminently a British enterprise and for years was the backbone of the merchant service. Chartered by one party at a time to run a single cargo, the tramp – of similar size to the cargo liner – was designed to perform as well as possible with varying cargoes on a maximum number of routes and to undertake to enter any sizeable port in the world. The competition for cargoes was intense, with the ever-present liability of being laid up for periods without work. By 1910 about half Britain's hugh mercantile marine consisted of tramp shipping. As with the cargo liners, however, deep-sea tramps were infrequent at Plymouth. At the turn of the century five were Plymouth owned, managed by J.A. Bellamy of Southside

First of the 'economy ships', designed by Sir Joseph Isherwood, the S.S. Arcwear
leaves the Sound for her steam trials off the Cornish coast, 1934.

Street, and registered in the port, but these were the exception, not the rule, and were probably based and maintained elsewhere.

THE ARCWEAR

After the slump of 1921 there was a marked decline in tramp shipping and great ingenuity was exercised by designers to make new tonnage cheaper to operate and so more competitive. To this period belong the innovations of the Isherwood arc-form hull, the Maierform bow, the Lentz and White steam engines and the Doxford diesel engine. The government introduced a 'scrap and build' loan scheme to subsidize new-style tramps provided two tons were scrapped for every one built. The Port of Plymouth contributed to the new tramp-ship era as the venue for the trials of the first 'arc-form' ship. The design was the brainchild of Sir Joseph Isherwood and in 1934 three ships of the type were built – *Arcwear*, *Arctees* and *Arcgow* – and the Arcwear Shipping Co. Ltd, London was formed to operate them. The *Arcwear* was the first completed, and came to Plymouth for her steam trials. She was a coal-burner of 7000 tons deadweight, designed to have a daily fuel consumption 15 – 20 per cent less than that of any comparable ship and to maintain a sea speed of 11 knots. On the voyage to Plymouth from Hull, where coal was loaded for Buenos Aires, an average speed of 11.15 knots was obtained. While at Plymouth the *Arcwear* was tested over the Polperro measured mile, averaging 12.1 knots, before leaving on her maiden voyage for Buenos Aires. The *Arcwear* was a handsome vessel with funnel amidships and holds fore and aft. Her dead weight capacity was greater and her resistance in the water less than any current tramp of similar size, and her rounded form of hull had a noticeable tumble-home. The second ship, *Arctees*, also visited Plymouth. On 23 January 1937, then renamed *English Trader*, she grounded on a reef outside Dartmouth harbour and was saved only by surgery; the floating stern was cut from the stranded bow and repaired by the building of a new bow section.

SOME EARLY MAILBOATS

The ocean mail and passenger liners which were to dominate the life of the port for nearly a hundred years began calling in the 1870s but had 'cast their shadow before'. For in 1838 the *Sirius* (the first ship to cross the Atlantic by steam throughout) called at Plymouth to land passengers and mail on her second eastbound passage; in 1845 Brunel's *Great Britain* embarked passengers at Plymouth on her way from London to Liverpool to make her first westbound crossing; while in 1850 the S.S. *Bosphorus* sailed from Plymouth with the first Cape Mails for South Africa. Before the turn of the century virtually all British and European liner companies serving the

S.P. Coy's Royal Mail liner La Plata *(ex* Calista, **4464 tons, 1882***) disembarking passengers and discharging baggage, mail and some cargo in Plymouth Sound using her own derricks, c. 1905.*

Americas, the Mediterranean, Africa and the Far East, were using Plymouth as a regular port of call.

ARRIVAL OF A LINER
The handling of a passenger liner's arrival in Plymouth Sound was a smooth-working and well-practised ritual. Passengers were embarked and disembarked – sometimes up to 800 at a time – by a tender. (The story of the tenders and the ocean terminals at Millbay Docks, and at Stonehouse Pool in 1904 – 11, is recounted in other booklets in this series.)

Practically all liners brought mail. It was off-loaded in sacks on to the tender, and at Millbay Docks fed by an electric conveyor belt straight into the sorting vans of a waiting 'Ocean Mails' express train.

Private cars (most numerous on the New York arrivals) were slung overside to the tender's wide deck, where up to twenty could be stowed. Many a humble docker could fantasize at the wheel of a Rolls or a Cadillac while positioning the car on deck or steering it ashore at the docks where it was given a 'Q' registration by the R.A.C. or A.A. man always in attendance.

Dogs were frequently landed, but had to be met with a licence and an

Typical scene from the hundred-year ocean liner era. The White Star Olympic, *sister of the ill-fated* Titanic, *leaves Plymouth under an overcast sky, 1919.*

approved portable kennel for transfer to quarantine. On the voyage dogs and other animals were invariably looked after by the ship's butcher.

Bullion was handled regularly; most Elder Dempster ships, for instance, brought gold specie. A proportion was examined ashore before all boxes were sealed and forwarded to the Bank of England, guarded, in those more honest days, by a single G.W.R. policeman!

To every incoming liner the G.P.O. sent a postman to collect telegrams, and Western Union sent a uniformed representative to collect cables.

PORT OF CALL

The Aberdeen & Commonwealth Line, plying to Australia via the 'Med', used Plymouth as a port of call for its 14 000 ton Bay-class steamers, built in 1921. Of these the *Jervis Bay* achieved undying fame as an armed merchant cruiser in the Second World War, when on 5 November 1940 she offered battle to the German pocket battleship *Admiral Scheer,* to allow her convoy to escape, and was sunk with all hands in the North Atlantic.

The Bergen Steamship Co. of Norway offered cruises from Plymouth on its 5 400 ton liner *Venus.* In March 1955, arriving from a cruise to Madeira and

Seen here at anchor in Plymouth Sound in 1938, the French liner Normandie *had a short career. Interned in the U.S.A. during the Second World War, she caught fire in New York harbour on 9 February 1942 and sank. She was raised only to be scrapped.*

about to depart on another, she went ashore at Jennycliff in the Sound in a southerly gale and took nearly a week to be refloated. Her bottom had been badly damaged by pounding in the swell, and Devonport Dockyard undertook the necessary repairs before she could go on her way.

Ships of the British India Steam Navigation Co. were a familiar sight in the Sound. Their passengers were principally British civil servants in East Africa. Frequent post-war callers were the M.V.s *Dwarka* and *Uganda*. When the *Dwarka* was withdrawn in the 1970s, her captain had the rare experience of being instructed by his company to run her hard aground – at the scrapyard! The school-cruise ship *Uganda* (1952, 16 907 tons) survived to give yeoman service as a hospital ship in the Falklands campaign, and has since been refitted.

None of the great companies was a better customer of Plymouth than the French line, Compagnie Générale Transatlantique, with its *Paris* (1921, 34 569 tons), *Ile de France* (1926, 43 450 tons) *Lafayette* (1929, 23 178 tons), *Champlain* (1932, 28 124 tons) and *Normandie* (1935, 86 496 tons). Frank Rushbrook, in his preface to *Fire Aboard*, claims that all passenger liners built before the Second World War were 'a floating fire risk of awful severity'. Certainly the C.G.T. was unlucky in this respect, *Lafayette* being destroyed by fire at Marseilles, *Paris* at Le Havre, and *Normandie* at New

Ile de France **(43 450 tons, 1926) leaving Plymouth c. 1952, photographed from the tender** Sir Richard Grenville (2). **In 1956 this veteran liner rescued 753 in the** Andrea Doria **disaster.**

York. The French line reduced its Plymouth calls in the late 1950s and withdrew altogether in 1961, which was a serious blow to the port.

The Cunard Steamship Co. called at Plymouth on its routes both to New York and Canada. Its 'crack' ships were household names in Britain – *Carmania, Lusitania, Mauretania, Aquitania, Berengaria* and *Queen Mary*. *Carmania* was the first large liner with turbine engines. As an armed merchant cruiser she fought, on 14 September 1914, the longest single naval engagement of the Great War against the German liner *Cap Trafalgar*, and sank her. *Lusitania* was torpedoed by the submarine U 20 off the Old Head of Kinsale on 7 May 1915, with the loss of 1198 lives. It was a special feature of the *Aquitania* that every stateroom or suite was decorated with reproductions of great paintings. *Berengaria* had been built in 1912 as the Hamburg-Amerika *Imperator* and was surrendered by Germany as part of her war reparations.

Queen Mary was completed in 1936. Started in 1930, work on 'No. 534' as she was called until her launch, was suspended for two and a quarter years because of an economic recession. Eventually the government advanced £4½ million to enable the ship to be completed, one condition being that the

The Cunard flyer Mauretania *leaving Plymouth, August 1929, photographed from the returning tender. She held the Blue Riband of the Atlantic for twenty-two years.*

Cunard-White Star R.M.S. Queen Mary arriving at Plymouth for the first time on 15 March 1937, after encountering gales and heavy seas on the crossing from New York.

Cunard Company should absorb the White Star Line. The new company of Cunard-White Star became effective from 1 January 1934. Not to upset White Star susceptibilities, a name with an '-ia' Cunard ending was eschewed; when on 26 September 1934 H.M. Queen Mary became the first British queen to launch a merchant vessel, she graced the ship with her own name.

The Hamburg-Amerika Line had been in the Western Ocean mail business from 1856. At the turn of the century it had the fastest ship in the world. The 16 502 ton *Deutschland* arrived in Plymouth from New York on 10 September 1910 after an unofficial but very real race with the then record holder *Kaiser Wilhelm de Grosse* for the Blue Riband. *Deutschland* had averaged 23.28 knots. HAPAG, as the line was commonly called, believed in 'putting on the style'. Between the wars its liners would arrive at Plymouth Breakwater with the ship's brass band playing on the boat deck.

The Holland-America line (1871) ran a mail and luxury passenger service to New York and enjoyed a high reputation with passengers. It absorbed the Red Star line of Antwerp in 1939. The very handsome *Nieuw Amsterdam* (1938, 36 287 tons), flagship of the line, was the largest Dutch merchant vessel. During the Second World War, *Spaarndam* was mined in the Thames estuary, *Statendam* burnt out in harbour and *Veendam* seized by the

Germans; but the remainder of the fleet became Allied troopships and resumed service after hostilities, when a new *Statendam* and *Rotterdam* were built in the late fifties.

Norddeutscher Lloyd produced, between 1897 and 1903, several handsome liners, with four funnels in pairs, and the company gained and retained the Blue Riband. In 1907 they lost the trophy to Cunard's *Lusitania*, regaining it by a narrow margin from the *Mauretania* twenty-two years later, with the 51 656 ton *Bremen*. A *Western Morning News* sailing notice of March 1913 shows how they advertised the final Plymouth – France and Germany stage of their return trips from New York. (See p.35.) *Bremen* was destroyed by bombing in the Second World War and her sister *Europa* transferred to France under war reparations in 1946.

The Henderson Line (P. Henderson & Co., Glasgow, 1871) carried first-class passengers only to Rangoon in Burma and Port Said in Egypt. Its *Amarapoora* and other principal liners were all 7500 – 8000 tonners, and all built by Denny of Dumbarton. They occasionally brought baulks of teak from Rangoon for H.M. Dockyard in the days when H.M. ships were decked with teak. It is a tribute to the company that a Henderson vessel was commonly chosen as Commodore's flagship when convoys were initiated in the Great War.

P. & O. (Peninsular & Oriental Steam Navigation Co., 1836) worked to India and Australia, calling at Plymouth when homeward bound, and – until 1936 – operated the 'P. & O. Branch Line' to Australia, calling outward bound at Plymouth. Famous ships included the *Kaiser-i-hind* (1914, 11 500 tons), five times attacked by U boats in the Great War, *Mooltan* (1923, 21 000 tons), *Rawalpindi* (1925, 16 619 tons) and *Rajputana* (1925, 16 568 tons) – these last two both torpedoed in the Second World War. A break with the traditional black hulls and brown upperworks was made with the introduction of the two 'white sisters' *Strathnaver* and *Strathaird*, introduced in 1931 and 1932 for the Australian service. They set the style and standards for the company's new vessels right up to the present-day *Canberra* of 1961.

The Union Castle Mail Steamship Co. Ltd (1853) had held the mail contract to Cape Town since 1857. Its red-and-black funnelled liners had lavender-grey hulls with reddish-brown boot topping. On 11 November 1890 a G.W.R. Cape Mail express which had met their incoming boat at Plymouth was wrecked in an accident at Norton Fitzwarren, fifty of the liner's passengers being killed. By the Second World War the company's eight principal mailboats were in the ratio of six motor to two steam.

United States Lines (1920), with red, white and blue funnels, operated two very successful 24 300 ton sister ships, *Washington* and *Manhattan*, as well as the 34 000 ton *America* and the giant *Leviathan* (1914, 59 957 tons), the ex-

A passenger liner, the *Black Watch,* with 360 people on board, limped into Plymouth Sound today after a nightmare voyage in which a freak giant wave smashed into the bridge, crippling vital controls and equipment.
WESTERN EVENING HERALD,
24 November 1984

German *Vaterland*, handed over as war reparation in 1919. The company's *United States* (1952, 53 329 tons), last of the Blue Riband winners, called only about four times at Plymouth, thereafter going to Southampton.

The White Star Line (Oceanic Steam Navigation Co. Ltd) brought many famous vessels to Plymouth Sound between 1870 and 1933, before merging with Cunard in 1934. These included *Majestic*, ex-*Bismarck* (1921, 56 551 tons), *Olympic* (1911, 46 430 tons), *Homeric* (1922, 34 351 tons) and the motor vessels *Britannic* and *Georgic*.

DECLINE OF LINER TRAFFIC

In the ten years before the Second World War P. & O. and other British lines began to build up a new industry of deep-sea cruises, the one sphere in which the subsidized foreign companies did not compete. They had such success that the figure of 20 000 cruise passengers in British ships in 1928 had risen to 62 500 before the war. Even so, no one then contemplated that the cruise liner would become a class of ship in its own right, and that the 'ferry' liner would pass from the scene. After the war the ocean liners began reappearing in the Sound as though the world had not changed, but with mail contracts being gradually transferred to airlines the writing was on the wall. When Great Britain, France and Holland started to give their colonies self-government in the 1950s, passenger traffic to the east dwindled to nothing once their civil servants had been brought home. Transatlantic traffic also evaporated as flying came into its own with comparable fares and short travelling time. Efforts to bring the cruising liners to Plymouth were unsuccessful. There is now a projected annual growth rate of 17 per cent for the cruising industry for the next few years, but, sadly, Plymouth it seems will have no part in it.

NEW CLASSES OF FREIGHTER

Ninety-five per cent of the world's international trade is still carried by sea, and *Jane's Merchant Shipping Review* gives nearly 80 000 seagoing ships in service in 1983. But the number of traditional cargo vessels, the only type with which Plymouth is equipped to deal, is dwindling rapidly. Not a week passes but more disappear to the breakers. The foreseeable future lies with new classes of freighters – bulk carriers, container ships and ro-ro (roll-on, roll-off traffic) vessels – all types requiring loading and discharging facilities

A post-war picture of the Spanish cruise liner Arosa Star of Vigo. Her engines are giving her slight sternway as she comes to anchor inside Plymouth Breakwater. An undated photograph.

which involve adequate hinterland to quays and good access to motorways and railways.

BROKERS AND AGENTS

No record of merchant shipping at Plymouth would be complete without some reference to the brokers and agents who arranged cargoes and bunkering, negotiated insurance, booked passengers and found crew replacements. After the Great War, takeovers and amalgamations took place in the interests of what it is now fashionable to call 'rationalization'. In April 1927 Wm Cory & Son Ltd opened an office in the Millbay Road headquarters of Weekes, Phillips & Co., aiming to sell coal to local industries on a contract basis. This was started by C.J. Moses, who until March that year had been in charge of ships' bunkering for Fox, Sons & Co. In 1929 Colonel F.R. Phillips of Weekes, Phillips & Co., approached Wm Cory & Son Ltd, F.C. Strick Ltd and Gray, Davies & Co. Ltd, proposing a merger: thus Cory & Strick Ltd was born. Phillips' motivation was the depression which resulted from the 1926 General Strike and the fact that Cory Colliers (coastal), Strick Line (grain carriers from the Persian Gulf) and the British India Line (passengers) were regular port users. Weekes, Phillips & Co. were bought out in this deal. Also taken over that year were Bellamy & Co., Cory Colliers' agents, and coal bunkering factors, while in 1930 the business of Fox, Sons & Co., P. & O. liner agents and bunkering factors, was acquired. After the Second World War Orlando Davies & Co. Ltd, agents for Bratt Line and others, were bought out by Cory & Strick Ltd, but continued trading under their original name until the Bratt Line ceased to call at Plymouth. In the 1950s G. Haswell & Co. Ltd opened a second office at Southampton because the French Line had started to use that port. When C.G.T. ceased calling at Plymouth, Haswell's was purchased by Cory & Strick Ltd in about 1961-2. Late in 1971 Wm Cory & Son bought out the Cory & Strick interests held by F.C. Strick Ltd and Gray, Davies & Co. Ltd, Cory & Strick thus becoming a wholly Wm Cory subsidiary. During 1972 all the agents purchased since 1929 were wound up, except Bellamy & Co. (Plymouth) Ltd, who took over all the agencies operationally. In 1974 Wm Cory & Son Ltd were bought out by Ocean Transport & Trading Ltd of Liverpool.

PLYMOUTH—CAPE REVIVAL

The most hopeful development in liner traffic came in 1983 with the unexpected revival of a Plymouth—Cape Town service. Inaugurated on 25 November that year by the Cornish firm Curnow Shipping, this was the first regular passenger service between Britain and South Africa since the

Curnow Shipping's World Renaissance, **12 000 tons, leaving Millbay Docks in November 1983 to inaugurate the short-lived revival of the Plymouth – Cape Town service.**

halcyon days of the famous Union Castle Line. The 12 000 ton French-built *World Renaissance* (passenger capacity 516) was timetabled to do the 6000 mile run in seventeen days, including calls at Cape Verde Islands and St Helena. Then, less than a fortnight before the first sailing, Safmarine, the South African shipping giant, announced a rival service from Southampton with the £33 million, 18 000 ton liner *Astor*. Curnow Shipping felt unable to compete with Safmarine's resources and announced that their service would terminate after April 1984 when the rival route was due to open. Millbay port manager Edward Chapman told the press he was 'very disappointed' by this news, as the liner was working from West Wharf, Millbay Docks, but promised 'we still intend to give it the best service'. However, when *World Renaissance* sailed on the inaugural trip with 250 passengers on a rainy afternoon, optimism was running high that the venture would be able to continue.

THE UNCERTAIN FUTURE

It is not easy to foresee a revival of merchant-shipping activity at Plymouth. No doubt coasters will continue to use the port as they have ever done, but the larger deep-water traders are another matter. The tendency today is towards sizeable freighters carrying greater payloads, and Plymouth's deep-water berths are few. Stonehouse Pool's Ocean Quay (16 ft LWOST*) is now a yacht marina; Cattewater's Turnchapel Wharf (18 ft LWOST) is held by the Ministry of Defence; and Victoria Wharves (24 ft LWOST) are largely monopolized by the important china-clay traffic. There remain Millbay's West Wharf (30 ft LWOST for 800 ft length) and Cattewater's Cattedown Wharves (26 ft LWOST for 1040 ft length). Neither has adequate hinterland for development. Moreover, neither has ideal access to the A38 for heavy vehicles. Cattedown has a somewhat run-down rail link; Millbay's connection with the main line has been obliterated. Yet the function of any major port in Britain is to receive the 'Big Steamers'. And the country is as dependent on them today as in the days of Kipling:

> For the food you eat and the biscuits you nibble,
> The sweets that you suck and the joints that you carve;
> They are brought to you daily by all us Big Steamers,
> And if anyone hinders our coming – you'll starve!

* Low water, ordinary spring tides.

N D L

Plymouth to Cherbourg (for Paris) and Bremen (for Harz mountains and Berlin) by the magnificent New York steamers of the Norddeutscher Lloyd.

Kaiser Wilhelm II	March 24
George Washington	March 29
Kronprinzessln Cecille	April 7
Prinz Friedrich Wilhelm	April 15

Fares to Cherbourg: 1st class 30/- 2nd Class 15/-
       to Bremen: 1st class £3 2nd class £2

Return to Southampton £5.8.0, 2nd class £3.12.0.

Passengers can Book on Steamships of this line from Bremen to all Stations on the Continent of Europe.

For further information and particulars apply to Orlando Davis & Co., 35 Southside Street, Plymouth.

Western Morning News **sailing notice of 12 March 1913**

Plymouth sail: fleet lists

William Pinkham & Co.

Amy	1868	146 t.n.
Eschol	1870	194 t.g.
Kitty Pinkham		
Polly Pinkham	1867	141 t.g.

W.H. Shilston & Co.

Countess of Devon	1873	232 g.	**Lily of Devon**	1868	396 g.
Earl of Devon	1876	449 g.	**Pride of Devon**	1867	358 g.
Elsa	1891	114 n.	**Rose of Devon**	1871	408 g.
Girl of Devon	1880	136 n.	**Western Lass**	1885	100 n.
Island Maid	1863	124 n.	**Antoinette**	1905	119 g.

John Westcott

Agnes	1854	122 n.	**Maren**	1876	170 n.
Amy	1870	126 n.	**Meridian**	1858	93 n.
Blanche	1873	74 n.	**Michael Kelly**	1871	138 n.
Constance Mary	1875	176 n.	**My Beauty**	1894	100 n.
Devon	1870	91 n.	**My Lady**	1889	93 n.
Ensign	1883	100 n.	**Nikita**	1890	97 n.
Esther	1856	79 n.	**Our Nellie**	1883	100 n.
Express	1885	90 n.	**Romola**	1872	80 n.
Fleetwing	1867	147 n.	**Rothersand**	1907	140 n.
Frances & Jane	1878	171 n.	**St Clair**	1890	97 n.
Ismene	1868	83 n.	**SPW**	1876	91 n.
John Sims	1873	98 n.	**Telephone**	1878	99 n.
Lilla	1870	76 n.			

Plymouth Mercantile Shipping Co.

Canterbury Bell	1876	60 n.	**JNR**	1893	41 n.
Eclipse	1892	32 n.	**Snowdrop**	1873	125 n.
Emma	1878	39 n.			

Davis & Stephens

Alfred Rooker	1876	70 n.	**Mouse**	1878	49 n.
Amy	1870	98 n.	**Regina**	1899	44 n.
Britannia	1896	39 n.			
Carrie Harvey	1881	111 g.			

Plymouth sail: fleet lists

W. Lawrey

Earl of Beaconsfield	1881	91 n.	**Pride of the West**	1880	99 n.
Mary Bassett	1864	80 n.	**Rose**	1890	77 n.

Tope family ships

Carmenta	1879	144 n.	**Louise Ernest**	1877	58 n.
Cicilia	1867	130 g.	**Twilight**	1878	120 g.
Dolphin	1867	120 n.	**Precursor**	1885	71 n.

Plymouth deep-sea steam tramps

Endsleigh	O.N. 97476	1891	2366 tons g.	Endsleigh S.S. Co., Plymouth
Lustleigh	O.N. 111359	1891	3250 tons g.	Cotehele S.S. Co., Plymouth
Maristow	O.N. 111343	1899	3506 tons g.	Maristow S.S. Co., Plymouth
Sir Richard Grenville	O.N. 99266	1892	2715 tons g.	Sir Richard Grenville S.S. Co., Plymouth
Sir Walter Raleigh	O.N. 95140	1889	1870 tons g.	Sir Walter Raleigh S.S. Co., Plymouth

Plymouth steam: fleet lists

Plym Shipping Company Ltd. 1947-58

Ship	Tons	Built	Engines	Speed
Alfred Plym	980	1937	Ruston 400 h.p.	
Janet Plym	375	1937	Petter diesel 360 h.p.	10 knots
Plympton	315	1937		
Plymstock	250	1937	Bronz 200 h.p.	8 knots
Rylands	250	1887	– Sail –	
Sunflower	1700		Oil burner	
Conlea	315	1944	Deutz 300 h.p.	10 knots
Fredor	785	1944	Atlas 500 h.p.	11 knots

Cornish Shipping Company Ltd

Ship	Tons deadweight	Built	Dimensions (ft)	Speed
Clafen	1024	1971	207 x 32½	12 knots
Cladyke	1024	1971	207 x 32½	12 knots
Peroto	805	1979	159½ x 29½	11 knots
Roy C	646	1971	162 x 29	10 knots
Emma	955	1951	197 x 30½	10 knots
Birte	490	1963	155 x 28	9 knots

Decline of British Shipping

Country	Percentage of steam & motor tonnage owned in the world		
	1901	1914	1939
Great Britain & Ireland	50.2	41.6	26.1
United States	4.2	4.5	13.0
Japan	2.2	3.8	8.2
Norway	3.4	4.3	7.1
Germany	10.1	11.3	6.5
Italy	2.7	3.1	5.0
France	4.4	4.2	4.3
Holland	2.1	3.2	4.3

M.V. World Renaissance

Built	Registered	Tonnage	Dimensions (ft)	Engines	Speed
1966 St Nazaire	Piraeus	12 000	492 x 68.9 x 37.7	2 oil 2 s.a. each 6 cy. — 13 680 b.h.p.	18 knots

Plymouth overseas passenger service

Company	Flag	Service	Some of the ships principally used	Approximate frequency	Operating period	Agents
Aberdeen & Commonwealth	Brit.	Australia via Suez Canal	**Esperance Bay Jervis Bay Largs Bay**		1920s & 1930s	
Alfred Holt & Co. Blue Funnel Line	Brit.	Hong Kong, Singapore & Far East	**Ulysses, Hector Laertes**	c. 8 weeks	Late 1800s–1960s	Fox Sons & Co. Bellamy & Co.
Bergen S.S. Co.	Nor.	Cruising	**Venus**	Weekly to Madeira	Nov.–March 1950–58	Weekes, Phillips & Co.
Bibby Bros. & Co.	Brit.	Suez, India & Far East (homeward)	**Dorsetshire Shropshire**	Fortnightly	1891–1939	
Blue Star Line	Brit.	South America	**Avila Star Arandora Star Almeda Star**	c. 8 calls a year	– 1955	Weekes, Phillips & Co.
British India S. Nav. Co.	Brit.	1. Mombasa, Beira, etc. 2. Calcutta	**1. Mantola Mulbera 2. Uganda, Kenya**	c. fortnightly	–1957	Gray, Dawes & Co.
City Line (Ellerman Group)	Brit.	Ceylon and Indian ports	**City of York City of Port Elizabeth**		–1956	Weekes, Phillips & Co. Haswell & Co.
Compagnie Générale Transatlantique	French	1. New York 2. W. Indies	**1. Normandie Paris Ile de France 2. Champlain Lafayette**		– 1958 – 1958	Haswell & Co.
Cunard S.S. Co.	Brit.	1. New York 2. Canada	**1. Mauretania Aquitania Queen Mary 2. Ascania Ausonia**	1. Every 10 days 2. Weekly	–1952	Cunard Line
Elder Dempster West Coast Boats	Brit.	West Coast of Africa	**Adda, Appam Abusso, Accra**		–1939	Travellers Ltd Coast Lines
Ellerman & Bucknall S.S. Co.	Brit.	South & East Africa	**City of Canberra City of Kimberley**			Weekes, Phillips & Co.
Ellerman Hall Line Ltd.	Brit.	Far East	**City of Glasgow, etc**	Monthly		Fox, Sons & Co.

Plymouth overseas passenger service						
Ellerman's Wilson Line Ltd	Brit.	Far East	**City of Ripon** **Urbino**			Fox, Sons & Co.
Hamburg-Amerika (HAPAG)	Ger.	West Indies	**Orinoco**	Fortnightly		W. H. Muller & Co.
Hamburg-South America	Ger.	South America	**Cap Arcona**	c. monthly		
Holland-America Line	Dutch	Rotterdam–New York–Plymouth	**Nieuw Amsterdam** **Veendam**	c. fortnightly	–1939	Bellamy & Co.
Jamaica Direct Fruit Line	Brit.	Kingston	**Jamaica Planter** **Jamaica Pioneer** **Jamaica Producer**	c. 6 weeks	After W.W. 2 c. 5 years	Weekes, Phillips & Co.
Johnson Line	Swed.	Vancouver	**Axel Johnson** **Annie Johnson**		1920s & 30s	
KNSM (Royal Netherlands S.S. Co.)	Dutch	Rotterdam–Plymouth –W. Indies	**Oranje Nassau** **Cottica, Willemstad**		1800s–1958	Bellamy & Co.
New Zealand Shipping Co.	Brit.	New Zealand (outward)	**Rotorua** **Rangitiki** **Rangitane**	Infrequent	1930–58	Fox, Sons & Co. Cory & Strick
Norddeutscher Lloyd	Ger.	New York (homeward)	**Deutschland** **Columbus, Bremen** **Europa**		– 1939	Orlando Davies & Co.
Orient Line	Brit.	Australia	**Oronsay** **Orsova** **Orontes**	Fortnightly	–1939	Cunard & Orient Lines
P. Henderson & Son	Brit.	Rangoon	**Yoma** **Pegu**		–1939	Weekes, Phillips & Co.
Pacific Steam Navigation Co. Ltd	Brit.	S. & Central America, Panama Canal	**Reina del Mar** **Reina del Pacifico**		–c. 1957	Travellers Ltd
P.&O.	Brit.	India, Australia (homeward)	**Kaiser-i-Hind** **Rawalpindi** **Strathnaver**	Weekly	–1939	Bellamy & Co.
P.&O. Branch Line	Brit.	Australia (outward)	**Ballaret** **Bendigo**	Monthly	1929–36	Weekes, Phillips & Co. Cory & Strick

Plymouth overseas passenger service						
Red Star Line	Brit.	New York	**Lapland** **Penland, etc.**	Tourist season only	–c.1933	
R.M.S.P. Co. Ltd.	Brit.	S. America	**Andes** **Asturias** **Alcantara**	c. 8/9 weeks	–1957	Coast Lines
Shaw, Savill & Co.	Brit.	Australia	**Dominion Monarch** **Ceramic**	Occasional calls	–1939	Weekes, Phillips & Co.
Union Castle Line	Brit.	South Africa	**Edinburgh Castle** **Windsor Castle**	Occasional calls	–1950	Coast Lines
United States Lines	U.S.A.	New York	**Leviathan** **Washington** **Manhattan**	c. fortnightly	1921–58	Orlando Davies Weekes, Phillips
White Star Line	Brit.	New York	**Majestic** **Olympic** **Homeric**		1907–26	Cunard & Orient Line
American Merchant Line	U.S.A.	New York	**American Banker** **American Farmer** **American Merchant**	Mostly tourist season		Weekes, Phillips & Co.
British & African S.N. Co.	Brit.					
President Line	U.S.A.	New York	**President Harding** **President** **Roosevelt**	Tourist season only	–c.1985	Weekes, Phillips & Co.

Plymouth home trade and narrow seas freight services

Company	Flag	Service	Some ships chiefly used	Approximate frequency	Operating period	Agents
Bratt (Gotha) Line	Swed.	Gothenburg–Plymouth–Bristol Channel Ports	**Adolf Consul Bratt Marianne**		c.1912 –c.1929	Orlando Davis
Bristol S.N. Co.	Brit.	Belgium, Holland Bristol Channel Ports	**Ino, Apollo Cato, Juno**	Weekly	–c. 1969	B.S.N. Co. with Fox, Sons & Co.
Bugsier Line	Ger.	Hamburg	**Wiedau**		Pre W.W. 2 and after 1969	Thos. Nicholson Cory & Strick
City of Cork S.P. Co.	Brit.	Waterford and Cork	**Macroom**		1892–1921	
Cork S.S. Co.	Brit.	Cork and London	**Citizen, Adonis Neptune**	Weekly	From 1850	Henry J. Waring
Cory Colliers	Brit.	Barry (coal)	**Corfen, Corbridge Corbrae**	Weekly	c.1900 –c.1955	Cory & Strick
Coast Lines Ltd	Brit	Liverpool & London	**Somerset Coast Ocean Coast**	Liverpool: twice a week. London: weekly.	c.1900– c.1957	Coast Lines
Coast Lines Ltd	Brit	Liverpool–Dublin –London	**Caledonian Coast Hibernian Coast**		1947–67	Coast Lines
Coast Lines (Langlands)	Brit	Scotland, W. Coast & S. Wales	**Highland Coast Cheshire Coast Lancashire Coast**		Until 1939	Coast Lines
Coast Lines	Brit.	Dublin & London (Guinness)	**Lady Wimborne Lady Cloe Lady Patricia**	Every Monday	Until 1939	Coast Lines
Coast Lines Ltd	Brit.	Silvertown, Torquay, etc. (sugar)	**M/V Fife Coast**			
Coast Lines Ltd	Brit.	Avonmouth (CWS flour)	Pre-war **Hampshire Coast** Post-war **Adriatic Coast**			Coast Lines

Plymouth home trade and narrow seas freight services						
Coast Lines Ltd	Brit.	Liverpool & South Coast ports (cattle foods)	(Whichever vessel available)	Irregular		Coast Lines
Coast Lines Ltd	Brit.	Blyth (coal)	(Whichever vessel available)			Coast Lines
Clyde Shipping Co. Ltd.	Brit.	Round Britain, westward and eastward	**M/V Rathlin** **M/V Eddystone**	Every Monday (W), every Saturday (E)		Clyde Shipping & Coast Lines
Esso Tankers	Brit.	Fawley (oil)	**Esso Poole** **Esso Chelsea**	2/3 days	1950s–1982	Bellamy & Co.
Holland Steamship Line	Dutch	Amsterdam– Plymouth–Bristol Channel Ports	**Ystroom** **Amstelstroom** **Vechtstroom**	Twice weekly	1920s–1939 1940s–1958	Haswell & Co.
Jersey Lines	Brit.	Jersey	**Ardenza** **M/V Tureby**	2 days		Weekes, Phillips
Moss-Hutchinson	Ger.	Bremerhaven		Monthly	Before and after W.W.2	Thos. Nicholson, Cory & Strick
Plymouth & Channel Islands Shipping Co.	Brit.	Channel Islands & Brittany	**New Verdun**	Weekly	Until c.1935	P.&C.I.S. Co.
Screw Steam Navigation Co.	Brit.	London, Ireland & Liverpool	**Pelican, Ajax** **Adlek**	Weekly	From c.1850– c.1890	Thos. Nicholson

Bibliography

Bridge Across the Atlantic Wallace Rayburn (Harrap)
British Shipping R.H. Thornton (Cambridge University Press, 1945)
British Ships and Shipping Peter Duff (Harrap, 1949)
Coastwise Sail Magazine (Files)
The Elements of Shipping Alan E. Branch (Chapman & Hall, 1977)
A Gateway of Empire C.M. Macinnes (Arrowsmith, 1968)
Jane's Merchant Shipping Review A.J. Ambrose
Lloyds Register of Shipping
The Maritime History of Devon M. Oppenheim (Exeter University, 1968)
Mercantile Navy List (H.M.S.O.)
The Merchant Schooners Vols 1 and 2 Basil Greenhill (National Maritime Museum, 1951)
Merchant Ships Talbot Booth (Sampson, Low, Marston & Co.)
Merchant Steamships Greenhill & Gifford (Batsford, 1979)
Plymouth: A New History Crispin Gill (David & Charles, 1979)
Plymouth, A Portrait J.C. Trewin (Hale, 1978)
Sea Breezes (Files)
Ships Monthly (Files)
Steam Coasters and Short Sea Traders C.V. Waine (Waine, 1976)
The Story of Plymouth R.A.J. Waller (Westaway, 1950)
Westcountry Coasting Ketches Slade & Greenhill (Conway, 1974)
Westcountry Passenger Steamers G. Farr (Stephenson, 1956)
Western Evening Herald (Files)
Western Morning News (Files)